ABRAHAM

Almighty God said:

"As for me, behold my c_ _ _ _ _ _ shall be a father of many nations.

Neither shall thy name any more be called Abram, but thy name shall be Abraham; for a father of many nations have I made thee.

And I will make thee exceeding fruitful, and I will make nations of thee, and kings shall come out of thee.

And I will establish my covenant between me and thee and thy seed after thee in their generations for an everlasting covenant, to be a God unto thee, and to thy seed after thee."

(Genesis 17:4-7)

Let it be noted that this Covenant was an Everlasting Contract. Concerning this Covenant it is said in Hebrews 6:13-20 that because God had sworn to it by an oath and because it was impossible for God to lie, the Covenant is immutable.

The Covenant was unalterable, unchangeable, and everlasting, which means IT MUST EXIST TODAY. Read the entire Covenant in Genesis 17, and you will find it not only concerned the ownership of all the land from the river Euphrates to the river Nile, but, overshadowing all else, it was a Covenant *"To be a God unto thee, and to thy seed after thee, in their generations for ever."* Can we comprehend what that means? It has not been revoked. Now note that the Covenant was made not only with Abraham for his lifetime but also with his seed forever, through Isaac (Gen. 17:8-24 and Romans 9:7-9) and through Isaac's son, Jacob. So we find the Everlasting Covenant made by Almighty God with Abraham, (Gen. 17:4-8) was established in Isaac, (Gen. 26:1-5) and was ratified and confirmed to Jacob. (Gen. 35:10-12)

Special attention must be called to the fact that the Covenant was absolutely unconditional, unalterable and unchangeable. It did not depend on what the descendants of Abraham did or did not do. The Covenant stands forever on the oath of God.

Abraham was also promised a tremendous number of descendants. Three symbols are used in Genesis to describe the number:

1. The dust of the earth:

"And I will make thy seed as the dust of the earth: so that if a man can number the dust of the earth, then shall thy seed also be numbered." (Gen. 13:16)

"And thy seed shall be as the dust of the earth, and thou shalt spread abroad to the west, and to the east, and to the north, and to the south: and in thee and in thy seed shall all the families of the earth be blessed." (Gen. 28:14)

2. The stars of heaven:

"And he brought him forth abroad, and said, Look now toward heaven, and tell the stars, if thou be able to number them: and he said unto him, So shall thy seed be." (Gen. 15:5)

3. The sand of the sea:

"That in blessing I will bless thee, and in multiplying I will multiply thy seed as the stars of the heaven, and as the sand which is upon the sea shore: and thy seed shall possess the gate of his enemies." (Gen. 22:17)

"And thou saidst, I will surely do thee good, and make thy seed as the sand of the sea, which cannot be numbered for multitude." (Gen. 32:12)

God later changed the name of Jacob to Israel, (Gen. 35:10) so his descendants who were the inheritors of the Covenant were hereafter known as Israel. Jacob had twelve sons, each the head of his own family. (Gen. 35:22-26) These families developed into the 12-tribed nation of Israel.

Jacob, (hereafter called Israel), loved Joseph more than all his other children. (Gen. 37:3) After the eldest son, Reuben, sinned against his father, (Gen. 35:22) Joseph, as the eldest son of Jacob and Rachel, inherited the **birthright** and special **blessing**. This made him the head of the family in regard to spiritual and secular affairs. Before Jacob-Israel died, Joseph brought his two sons to his father to receive the **blessing** and the **birthright**. (I Chron. 5:1) Israel crossed his hands and laying his hands on their heads, blessed the sons of Joseph – Ephraim and Manasseh. He then said, *"And let my name be named on them."* Thus his adoption of the two sons of Joseph created another tribe, making thirteen tribes in all. Although Joseph was displeased that his father's right hand was laid upon the head of Ephraim, the younger brother, Israel refused to uncross his hands, so Ephraim was set before Manasseh. (Gen. 48:13-20) Thus Manasseh became the thirteenth tribe and received the promise of becoming a **GREAT nation**. Ephraim was given the promise of becoming a **company of nations**. (Gen. 48:19)

Much of the history of the now thirteen tribes of Israel must, of necessity, be passed over here. The dramatic account of their sojourn in the land of Egypt for over 400 years, their great deliverance by the hand of God from the land, and the still greater deliverance at the Red Sea when God caused the waters to stand back while He led His people across on dry land to safety can be found in Exodus, chapters 1-14.

Finally, at Mount Sinai, God gave His people a code of Laws, Statutes, Judgments, Commandments and Ordinances (the latter ceased with the crucifixion and resurrection of Jesus Christ) by which His Kingdom on earth would be administered. (Exodus, chapters 19-40, and the books of Leviticus, Numbers and Deuteronomy) These laws covered every phase of both national and individual life: social, financial, economic, ecclesiastical, agricultural, dietetic, and personal.

The keeping of these laws, based on the promise and the assurance of God, will result in perfect happiness and contentment with freedom from sickness. Concerning these laws, the Psalmist wrote: *"The law of the Lord is perfect."* (Psalm 19:7)

The people at Mt. Sinai entered into a solemn covenant with their God and King, for they said, *"All that the Lord hath spoken we will do."* (Exodus 24:7) That is what is known as the first or National Covenant, and must not be confused with the Abrahamic Covenant which was made some four hundred years previously and which was unconditional. The Covenant made at Mt. Sinai was made conditional upon the keeping of the Laws, Statutes, Judgments and Commandments of God.

So we find God laying before His people the conditions of this National Covenant. IF they kept His laws, blessed would they be in all their undertakings: blessed in the city and in the field, in the fruit of the ground, in their cattle and flocks, in assurance of certain victory over their enemies, and in health and prosperity among the people. BUT, if they did not keep those laws, then the opposite would be the result. All their undertakings would be cursed: there would be crop failures, diseases in cattle and in their own bodies, poverty and sickness would overtake them, and their enemies would gain the victory in battle. All this may be read in Deuteronomy, chapter 28, and in Leviticus, chapter 26.

Here, God warned Israel that if they persisted in continually breaking His Laws, not only would curses come upon them, but He would punish them for seven times, (a time being 360 years, seven times would be 2520 years). They would be banished from the land of Palestine and scattered among the heathen (like lost sheep). (Lev. 26:28-46)

After entering the Promised Land the people obeyed the laws of the kingdom and received the promised rewards. All went well for many years. Then they began to tire and

–4–

wanted to be like other people around them. First of all they desired an earthly king, and God said that although in doing so they had rejected Him, He would give them permission to have an earthly king. (I Sam. 8:7-22) Saul was then appointed as Israel's first king.

Later he was removed because of sin, and God Himself appointed David (of the tribe of Judah) to be King over all Israel. God then established an Everlasting Covenant with David that his throne and his house would endure FOREVER as long as the sun and the moon endured in the heavens, (II Sam. 7:11-17 and Psalm 89:3-4,29-37) and that there would always be one of David's seed of lineage to reign upon that throne over the House of Israel forever. (Jer. 33:17-26)

So here we have:

(1) The Everlasting Covenant made with the Israel people through their forefathers, Abraham, Isaac and Jacob, whom God named "Israel."

(2) The Kingdom of Israel established forever.

(3) The Throne and the House of David established as the Monarchical system over the House of Israel forever.

So the House of Israel, the Throne of David, and the Everlasting Covenant must be in existence TODAY. Note: The throne of David was also the Throne of the Lord, (I Chron. 29:23) and will yet be occupied by the risen Christ, the King of Israel, *"For the Lord God shall give unto Him the Throne of His Father David, and He shall reign over the House of Jacob forever."* (Luke 1:32-33) Remember, He has not as yet occupied that Throne.

To return to David's reign, we find that he reigned for seven years over the House of Judah only, and then for thirty-three years over all Israel, (namely thirteen-tribed Israel - II Sam. 5:4-5). During his reign, while Israel kept the Laws of

God, prosperity was the result. Of that time it is recorded, *"Every man dwelt safely under his own vine and fig tree."* (I Kings 4:25) A perfect social order existed wherein dwelt righteousness.

So wonderful and glorious was the Kingdom that kings and queens came from all parts of the earth to see the glories of the kingdom. But alas, Solomon, who succeeded his father David to the throne of Israel, began to sin against God, causing the people of the thirteen tribes to sin. As a result of their sin, God then divided the kingdom into *two* kingdoms. (I Kings 11:29-36) The *ten tribes* under the leadership of Ephraim formed the Northern Kingdom of Israel with Samaria as their capital and Jeroboam as their king.

The other *two tribes* of Judah and Benjamin, with most of the tribe of Levi, formed what was known as the Southern Kingdom of Judah, with their capital located at Jerusalem, and Rehoboam as their king. (I Kings 12:16-20) Although Judah had received a large part of the tribe of Levi, she was still referred to as the two-tribed kingdom. The tribe of Levi, having received no inheritance with Israel, (Deut. 18:1-2) was portioned among all the tribes for priestly duties. This did not remove Levi from being a distinct tribe, only from being numbered among the landed tribes. Although Scripture thereafter refers to the "Twelve tribes," or the "ten-tribed" and "two-tribed" kingdoms, Manasseh remained numbered as the thirteenth tribe.

The titles "House of Israel" and "House of Judah" are used to designate the two kingdoms, as they stand separated and in opposition to each other.

The "Birthright" tribes, Ephraim and Manasseh, were included in the ten-tribed kingdom (House of Israel), while the tribe of Judah (to whom pertains the Throne or "Sceptre" through God's Covenant with David) was part of the two-tribed kingdom (House of Judah). The **SCEPTRE** and the **BIRTHRIGHT** were separated then and there. (I Chron. 5:2)

Each became a nucleus. All the seed of Abraham, Isaac and Jacob gathered around either one or the other.

The Divided Kingdom

The Northern Kingdom, "Israel," 933-721 B.C.

The Southern Kingdom, "Judah," 933-606 B.C.

The King of Judah assembled his army together to use force to unite the kingdoms, but God forbade it, saying He had divided the Kingdoms. (I Kings 12:21-24) Thus, each was free and independent of the other to fulfill their God-appointed destiny: one to fulfill the first covenant which the Lord made with their father Abraham, that of having multitudinous seed, spreading abroad and becoming many nations having kings over them; the other to fulfill the second covenant of bringing forth the Messiah.

After the division of Israel into two kingdoms, the people went deeper and deeper into sin. Finally the warning which God had given them in Leviticus 26, that if they persisted in sinning He would invoke the seven times punishment and cause them to be removed from their land and scattered among the heathen, was put into effect. The Assyrians came against the Northern Kingdom (ten-tribed Israel), and defeating them in battles, carried them away captive into Assyria. They were put into Halah, and in Habor by the river Gozan, and in the cities of the Medes. In one final invasion the balance of the Northern Kingdom was removed into exile. The accounts of the invasions may be found in II Kings 17:6-18 and 18:11-12. Some of the tribes had been removed in previous invasions by Assyria. (II Kings 15:29)

The cities of Samaria, once occupied by the people of the Northern Kingdom, were then re-populated by the Assyrians with captive people from Babylon, from Cuthah, from Ava, from Hamath and from Sepharvaim. (II Kings 17:24) These captives, not of Israel, were the Samaritans referred to by Jesus when He commanded His disciples to go not into the cities of the Samaritans, but go rather to the lost sheep of the House of Israel. (Matt. 10:5-6)

Note that the term "House of Israel," after the captivity of both kingdoms, often was applied to all the thirteen tribes collectively, including Judah. Sometimes the word "whole" House of Israel, House of Israel "wholly" and "all Israel" were used.

In spite of the terrible experiences of the House of Israel, strange to say, the House of Judah did not learn their lesson or heed the warning, for the Scripture states that they continued in sin even more than the Northern Kingdom. (Jer. 3:6-11) So we find the same punishment being meted out to them, starting with a series of invasions by Sennacherib, King of Assyria, (II Kings 18:13) when a greater part of Judah was also carried away captive to Assyria. This was followed later by the invasions of Nebuchadnezzar, King of Babylon. On these latter occasions, the captives of Judah were carried away to Babylon until finally they had all been removed from the land of Palestine. (II Kings 24:1-4 and 24:11-14) The third invasion (II Kings 25:1-12) and then the final removal (II Kings 25:22-26) fulfilled God's warning to them in Leviticus, chapter 26.

This is where the modern churches fail to fully understand the Scripture. They declare that because God had caused Israel to be driven from the land of Palestine, He had cast them away forever. In doing so, they teach, God had brought His Kingdom, established at Mount Sinai, to an end, and in its place had chosen what they term the Gentile church, or "Spiritual Israel."

In contradiction to this theory, God is faithful. He cannot and will not lie, and He will keep His Everlasting Covenant made with Abraham and his descendants, Israel. For if He has cast His people away forever and they no longer exist, then God has lied and He has been unfaithful. He has broken His Everlasting Covenant with them and is not dependable. But we know He does not and cannot lie. (Heb. 6:18)

No evidence can be found in Scripture that God has cast away His people forever. The proofs that God has not cast them off are too numerous to be listed here, but a few should be mentioned. Read Leviticus 26, where God warned Israel that the result of continued sinning would be removal from their land to be scattered throughout the nations of the earth.

But in the 44th verse we have God's definite statement that even when they were in the hands of their enemies He would not cast them away. Even for all their sin, He would not break His Covenant with them. This is repeated in Deut. 4:26-31.

Again in Isaiah 41:8-9, after all Israel had been scattered, God says He has not cast them away. Then in the closing book of the Old Testament, Malachi 3:6, God says to Israel, *"I am the Lord, I change not; therefore ye sons of Jacob are NOT consumed."*

We also find in the New Testament when Christ, the God of Israel, came to earth, He declared: *"I am not sent, but unto the lost sheep of the house of Israel."* (Matt. 15:24) Would He have come to seek a people that did not exist? Rather, it is declared of Him that He came to *"confirm the promises made unto the fathers."* (Rom. 15:8)

Also, Paul, in answer to the question, *"Hath God cast away his people"?* replied in no uncertain terms, *"God hath not cast away his people."* (Rom. 11:1-2) The Epistle of James is addressed *"to the twelve tribes which are scattered abroad."* Peter wrote to the strangers and pilgrims in the lands through which they were scattered. (I Peter 1:1,2) A wealth of Scripture can be found to prove that God has sworn He will never cast away His Israel people or break His Everlasting Covenant with them.

Our Lord Jesus Christ, Paul, Peter, James, and the prophets all declare they were *not* cast away, but most churches of today teach that God has cast them away forever, thereby nullifying His Everlasting Covenant with them. Whom do you believe? If you really believe God, then there can be only one answer, and that is the answer given by Paul, *"God hath not cast away his people."* What then became of them?

Numerous passages of Scripture could be presented to answer this question, but due to the brevity of this book only a few will be given here.

We will start with the Prophet Jeremiah, and in Jer. 31:10 he writes: *"And declare it in the isles afar off, and say, He that scattered Israel will gather him, and keep him, as a shepherd doth his flock."* That was a promise made by God to Israel after their dispersion; it is confirmed again in Jer. 32:37-44, then again in Isa. 43:5-6, addressed to scattered Israel. In Jeremiah 18, God tells the prophet that *just as the potter's clay was marred in the hands of the potter, but was taken again the second time and remolded into a perfect vessel, so would He do with the House of Israel.* In Jer. 46:27, God told Israel He would save them from afar off, together with all their seed. And in Ezekiel 20:34, God promised to gather Israel out of the countries wherein they were scattered.

In Amos 9:9, God declared that although He will sift Israel among the nations *"like as corn is sifted in a sieve, yet shall not the least grain fall upon the earth."* Then in the 14th and 15th verses He once again promised to bring them to their own land in the appointed time, where they *"shall no more be pulled up out of their land which I have given them."*

Israel was to be divorced from the Mosaic Law, and their identity temporarily lost to history, but known to God. They were to be recovenanted, in Christ, to enjoy the Israel Birthright in the "appointed" land; *"Moreover I will appoint a place for my people Israel, and will plant them, that they may dwell in a place of their own, and move no more, neither shall the children of wickedness afflict them any more, as beforetime."* (II Sam. 7:10) Since the children of Israel were in Palestine at the time this prophecy was given, it follows that the appointed place had to be somewhere else.

In Ezekiel 34:1-16, God sees His sheep, His people Israel, *"scattered upon all the face of the earth,"* as lost sheep without a shepherd, and the 11-12th verses state, *"For thus saith the Lord God, Behold I, even I, will both search my sheep, and seek them out. As a shepherd seeketh out his flock in the day that he is among his sheep that are scattered; so will I seek out my sheep, and will deliver them out of all places where they have been scattered in the cloudy and dark day."*

Here, God is saying that He Himself would come and seek them out as a shepherd seeking his lost sheep, (Jer. 31:10) and when Christ came to earth He said, *"I and my Father are one."* (John 10:30) Timothy understood this great mystery and stated, *"God was manifest in the flesh, justified in the Spirit, seen of angels, preached unto the Gentiles*, believed on in the world, received up into glory."* (I Tim. 3:16) Clearly this was referring to Christ of whom the prophets foretold, *"He would be called the Son of God."* St. Matthew also understood what was spoken of the Lord by the Prophet Isaiah, *"Behold, a virgin shall be with child, and shall bring forth a son, and they shall call his name Emmanuel, which being interpreted is, God with us."* (Matt. 1:23) Isaiah also gave among the names of the child, *"The Everlasting Father."* (Isaiah 9:6)

Christ then openly declared: *"I am not sent but unto the lost sheep of the house of Israel"* (Matt. 15:24); *"I am the good shepherd: the good shepherd giveth his life for the sheep"* (John 10:11); *"The Son of Man is come to save that which was lost."* (Matt. 18:11) He commissioned His disciples, *"As the Father hath sent me even so send I you."* A study of the Epistles will soon prove that they have found Israel where they had been scattered throughout Western Europe and part of Asia, and in the Isles of the Sea, north and west of Palestine.

*Gentile - To better understand what Timothy said it must be pointed out that the word "Gentile," which is not to be found in any original Scripture, is a translated word from the Greek word "ethnos" which means "heathen," "people" or "nations." The word could have been translated "people" or even better "nations," for Christ did not go to the heathen but rather He did preach to the people or nations of Israel as will be shown later.

Now, what is the purpose of the re-gathering of Israel? The answer from Scripture is that God may keep His Everlasting Covenant with them made through their forefathers Abraham, Isaac and Jacob. Therefore, He is going to restore His Kingdom on earth with Israel, once again, as His subjects.

Read what the prophets have to say on this subject of the re-gathering of Israel. Isaiah, from the 40th chapter to the end, is filled with the promises of God to Israel in the Isles of the sea and then to America (the place of His Kingdom on earth, the **New JerUSAlem**. At the second advent of Christ, He shall take the Throne. (Luke 1:32) Jeremiah has much to say concerning the promise of the restoration of Israel and Judah. See Jeremiah, chapters 30, 31, and 32. Ezekiel, from the 36th through the 39th chapters gives the plans or blueprints for the restoration of the kingdom. In Ezekiel 37:16-17 the divided kingdom, referred to as the "sticks" of Judah and Ephraim, is joined into one "stick." God clearly explains the meaning of this in verse 22 that the divided kingdom shall once again become one kingdom or nation with one king. And both the prophets Zechariah and Joel tell about the restored kingdom.

In the 23rd chapter of Jeremiah, God pronounces woe upon the false pastors who have destroyed and scattered His sheep. But in the 3rd verse is the promise that He will gather His flock out of all the countries whither He had driven them and would bring them again to their folds: *"And I will set up shepherds over them which shall feed them; and they shall fear no more, nor be dismayed, neither shall they be lacking, saith the Lord. Behold, the days come, saith the Lord, that I will raise unto David a righteous Branch, and a King shall reign and prosper, and shall execute judgment and justice in the earth."* (Jer. 23:4-5)

Who is this new King? – None other than Jesus the Christ, the living God. *"In his days, Judah shall be saved, and Israel shall dwell safely: and this is his name whereby he shall be called, THE LORD OUR RIGHTEOUSNESS."* (Jer. 23:6)

Yes, Jesus Christ "THE KING." Remember what was read in Luke 1:32-33: *"And the Lord God shall give unto him the throne of his father David. And he shall reign over the house of Jacob for ever; and of his kingdom there shall be no end."* And also Isaiah 9:6-7, *"For unto us a child is born, unto us a son is given: and the government shall be upon his shoulder: and his name shall be called Wonderful, Counselor, The mighty God, The everlasting Father, The Prince of Peace. Of the increase of his government and peace there shall be no end, upon the throne of David, and upon his kingdom, to order it, and to establish it with judgment and with justice from henceforth even forever. The zeal of the Lord of hosts will perform this."*

Yes, the risen Christ is going to return to take the Throne of David, and to reign over the House of Jacob forever with the whole thirteen tribes restored.

This was made possible when Israel was redeemed without money after having sold themselves for naught. (Isaiah 52:3) The 53rd chapter of Isaiah tells of the Redeemer and the terrible price He would have to pay to redeem His people from their sins, even to the shedding of His precious blood there on Calvary to make an atonement for His people. Yes, *"He was wounded for OUR transgressions, he was bruised for OUR iniquities: the chastisement of our peace was upon him; and with his stripes we are healed."* (Isaiah 53:5)

Yes, Jesus, the Christ, the Shepherd of His sheep, came to seek and save the lost sheep of the House of Israel, and give His life for His sheep. On Calvary's cross He redeemed them and saved them from their sins, but He rose again on the third day, triumphant over death. Thereby He opened the way to eternal life to all who would believe on His name. He ascended into Heaven, *"From henceforth expecting till his enemies be made his footstool."* (Heb. 10:13) When He returns

He will take the Throne of David and reign over the House of Jacob forever.

This wonderful promise of the restoration of Israel and Judah will be preceded by a great cleansing, and God Himself has undertaken to do that. God gives us the details of this in Ezekiel 36:16-38, and you will notice in verses 22 and 32 that God declares He is not doing it for Israel's sake but for His own Holy Name's sake. In verse 37 He says these words, *"Thus saith the Lord God; I will yet for this be inquired of by the house of Israel, to do it for them."* Then Israel will be made ready to receive her King.

Now, going back to the delivering or gathering of Israel to a new land as prophesied by Jeremiah, we read: *"And I will gather the remnant of my flock out of all countries whither I have driven them, and will bring them again to their folds; and they shall be fruitful and increase."* (Jer. 23:3) Also, *"But, the Lord liveth, which brought up and which led the seed of the house of Israel out of the north country, and from all countries whither I had driven them; and they shall dwell in their own land."* (Jer. 23:8) This began with the fall of the Assyrian Empire when portions of the tribes started across Europe toward the Isles in the Sea. Many were yet in the area of their captivity, even until the days of Christ. At the time of the Apostles, when upon the commandment of Christ to *"Go not into the way of the Gentiles, and into any city of the Samaritans enter ye not: But go rather to the lost sheep of the house of Israel,"* (Matt. 10:5-6) they went into these areas seeking the "lost sheep," the exiled tribes. This was the fulfillment of the Scripture, *"Yet does He devise means, that his banished be not expelled from Him."* (II Sam. 14:14) In keeping with the Scripture, the Apostles went into the cities of the Medes, Galatia, Halah, Pamphylia, Cappadocia and the region of the Euxine Sea.

From these areas in Media and northern Mesopotamia, the Israelites were taken (between 745-700 B.C.) and became the so-called Lost Tribes of Israel. After a lapse of over 2,500 years, it might be thought that all hope of tracing the Israelites had been lost in the midst of antiquity. But archaeologists have, during the last hundred years, unearthed and published the original contemporary records of the Assyrians who took the Israelites captive, and it is from these records that vital clues have come to light. The clues, in the form of cuneiform tablets, identify the lost Israelites with the Assyrian name "Gimira." They further recorded their migrations out of Asia Minor.

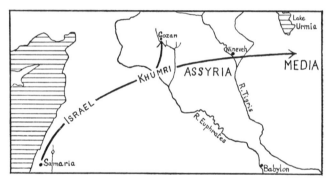

732-700 B.C. Israel taken into exile by the Assyrians who called them Khumri, later corrupted to Gimira.

The Assyrian records reveal one group of Gimira (Israelites) escaped to the shore of the Black Sea during the second year of Esarhaddon, 679 B.C. After raiding Lydia and settling there for awhile, the Israelites crossed the Black Sea to the Carpathian region, called in 2nd Esdras "Ar-sareth," or "Mountains of Sereth." The Greeks called these Gimira, "Kimmerioi," translated into English, "Cimmerians." It is also mentioned in 2nd Esdras 13:40-44 that some of the tribes of Israel made their escape into the mountains of Asia Minor by way of the upper Euphrates gorge.

710-590 B.C. Israelites called Gimira by the Assyrians and Cimmerians by the Greeks established a reign of terror in Asia Minor. They finally migrated to Europe to a place which they called Arsareth. (2 Esdras 13:40-44)

The larger body of Israelites, who had not escaped the Assyrians, were later allowed to establish colonies in Sacasene and Bactria. These colonies were first called "Gimira" but later

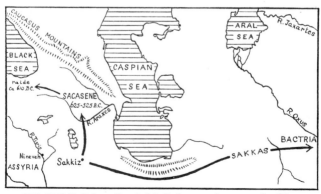

650-600 B.C. Israelites in Media became known as Scythians.

"Iskuza" by the Assyrians. After the fall of the Assyrian capital Nineveh in 612 B.C. to the Medes and Babylonians, the Gimira colonies were driven out of Media. The colony of Sacasene passed through the Dariel Pass in the Caucasus Mountains and occupied the steppe regions of South Russia. The colony of Bactria retreated across the Jaxartes River eastward into Central Asia, some going east as far as the borders of China.

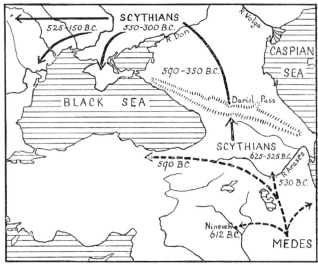

600-500 B.C. Following the collapse of their Assyrian allies, the Scythians were driven north through the Caucasus by the Medes, and settled in South Russia.

A rock-hewn inscription at Behistun, in North Persia, shows the Persian equivalent for Gimira was "Sakka," probably derived from "Isaaca," or house of Isaac; the name by which the Israelites called themselves. (Amos 7:9,16) Ancient historians tell us that the people whom the Greeks called "Scythians" were called "Sacae" or "Sakka" by the Persians. The Greeks got the name "Scythian" from the Assyrian "Iskuza," which is quite probably derived from Isaac.

During the fifth century B.C., the Scythian Israelites began moving across the rivers Don and Dnieper, thus coming into collision with the Cimmerian Israelites who had earlier migrated round the west of the Black Sea. Knowledge of their kinship having been lost during the centuries of separation, battles ensued, forcing the Cimmerians west. Some moved away to the north-west into the sparsely inhabited regions of the Baltic, where they later became known to the Romans as "Cimbri." The larger body of Cimmerians migrated as scattered bands up the Danube River, arriving near its source in South Germany about 600-500 B.C. There they became known as "Celts" and "Gauls." They gave the lower Danube the Celtic name "Ister," meaning lowness.

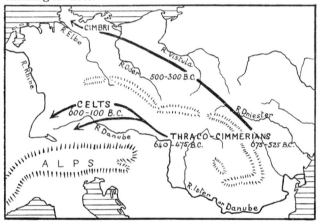

650-500 B.C. Cimmerians in Europe moved up the Danube and became known as Celts.

525-300 B.C. Others driven out of South Russia by the Scythains moved north-west between the rivers Oder and Vistula to the Baltic, where they later became known as Cimbri.

About 390 B.C., some of the Cimmerian Israelites invaded Italy and sacked Rome. About 280 B.C. others invaded Greece, and as they migrated back into Asia Minor they were called "Galatians" by the Greeks. However, most of them spread west and north across France and began to cross the English Channel into the British Isles.

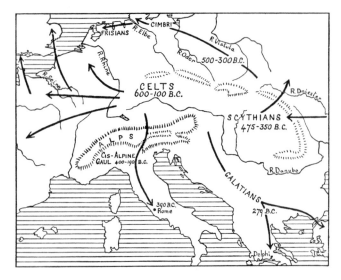

400-100 B.C. The Celtic expansion from Central Europe: some attacked Rome in 390 B.C. and settled for 200 years in northern Italy; others known as Galatians, after invading Greece in 279 B.C., migrated to Asia Minor. Most of them moved west into France and later to Britain.

From the fifth to the fourth century B.C., the Scythian Israelites established themselves in South Russia as the great and prosperous kingdom of Scythia. They formed close trade relations with the Greeks whom they supplied with grain. Toward the end of the third century, however, a non-Israelitish people, the Sarmatians, swept into South Russia from the east. By the end of the second century B.C., they had occupied all the Carpathian regions and the Danube. Only two small pockets of Scythians were left on the shores of the Black Sea; one in the Crimea and the other south of the Danube delta. Squeezed between Sarmatians and Celts, the main body of Scythians were driven north-west, where they were later reported by the Romans as occupying the south coast of the Baltic and North Seas.

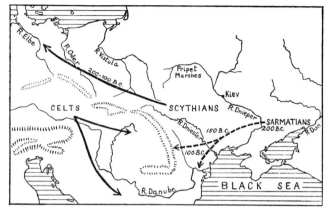

250-100 B.C. South Russia was invaded from the east by the Sarmatians, who drove the Scythians north-west through Poland into Germany.

As the Sarmatian tribes moved into "Scythia" in South Russia, there was a tendency to confuse them with the Scythians, but the Romans introduced the name "German" for the genuine Scythians (*germanus* being Latin for genuine). Except in outlying parts, the name Scythian was dropped in favor of Germans and Sarmatians. Nevertheless, the land south of the Baltic and eastern North Sea was still called Scythia, and as late as A.D. 800 the old Welsh historian, Nennius, called the home of the Anglo-Saxons, "Scythia."

It is well known that the Anglo-Saxons who came to Britain were called Germans by the Romans, and the Normans, who were the last to arrive in A.D. 1066, were of the same stock.

As the Scythians were driven west by the Sarmatians, they in turn drove the Cimbri across the Rhine into France. The Cimbri, in search of living area, went roving and pillaging as far as Spain and Italy, but were almost entirely wiped out in battles with the Romans. One group did reach North Britain by ships, and became known as the "Picts."

Between 400-100 B.C., the Celts continued to pour into Britain to form the "bed-rock" of the British race. One group in Spain, known as "Iberes" (the Gaelic name for Hebrews), moved into Ireland as "Scots," naming the island "Hibernia"; a name that still exists. Some Celts remaining in Spain became known as "Basques"; others in France became known as "Bretons."

During the succeeding centuries the Scythian Germans broke up into many divisions, possibly in some instances into their original Israel tribal families. One group settled around the shores of the Baltic Sea as "Goths." Others became the Angles, Saxons, Jutes, Danes and Vikings, to name just a few. Later, other Germanic tribes poured into the lands vacated by the Celts and established the Gothic nations of the Vandals, Lombards, Franks, Burgundians and Ostrogoths.

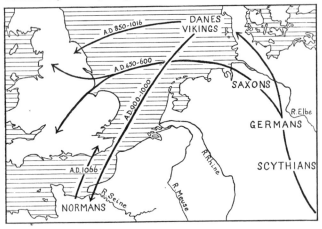

450-1100 A.D. The Romans re-named the Scythians, Germans. Some of these came to Britain as Anglo-Saxons, A.D. 450-600; others, after moving north through Jutland, became known as Danes and Vikings. Some of these came directly to England, but others settled for a short time in France and were called Normans.

The tribes, as they migrated westward, mixed with a great number of Israelites who had left their homeland long before the captivities began. They had migrated due to overpopulation of their homeland, and later for fear of the then rising Assyrian Empire. The people of Dan (one of the tribes of Israel) were explorers and settled in new places. Centuries before the captivities they founded colonies in Greece, which attracted immigrants from the other tribes. The Bible speaks of Zebulun and Naphtali as being great warriors. The blond Hellenes (early Greeks) were noted for strong, healthy bodies. Many years later, when Greece brought home dark-skinned slaves and intermarried with them, the modern olive to dark-skinned black-haired Greek was developed. Early Troy was founded by Israelites that came from Egypt before the Exodus (1453 B.C.). From Troy came the Romans who settled in Italy.

The Israelites, when reaching the "Isles of the West," found that descendants of Judah's twin son Zarah (Zarahites who had never entered the land of Palestine) had preceded them. The authenticated arrival to the Isles of Brutus the Trojan in 1103 B.C. and his founding of the ancient city of London, first called New Troy, is also of the branch of Judah. They, too, had previously absorbed peoples known as the early Aryan-Phoenicians, who had settled in the Isles over a thousand years prior, under the leadership of Hu Gadarn. Besides their stone monuments (among which are Stonehenge and Avebury) and their names, we have only traditional records of them.

The similarity of stone groupings and astronomical alignments of the monuments found in Brittany with those of the peoples of early Asia is one link in the mass of evidence unearthed by biblical archaeologists in tracing these older Hebrew-Phoenicians to the area where the Adamic or Aryan race originated, near the Pamir Plateau in Central Asia, an area that satisfies the geography of the first chapters of Genesis. These early Hebrew-Phoenicians were referred to as "Tarshish" by ancient records as well as Bible Scriptures.

Isaiah wrote, *"Surely the isles shall wait for me, and the ships of Tarshish first, to bring thy sons from far."* (Isaiah 60:9) And again, *"I will send those that escape of them unto the nations, to Tarshish, Pul, and Lud* [an old name for London], *that draw the bow, to Tubal, and Javan, to the isles afar off."* (Isaiah 66:19) Ezekiel also wrote of the *"merchants of Tarshish."* (Ezekiel 38:13)

Going back to God's warning of the seven times punishment to be meted out to Israel if she persisted in sinful ways, it is logical to assume that the starting date of that punishment period would begin from the date of the removal of Israel from her homeland in Palestine.

A study of the dates when the various tribes were taken into captivity will show that they were not all taken captive at one time. In fact, history records a difference of many years in their captivities. Thus, the punishment period of 2520 years would start and end at different times depending on the **tribe** of Israel. Now by adding 2520 years to the starting date of each of the tribes of Israel going into captivity, where such dates are available, one can establish the ending date of the punishment period. Not all of the exact starting dates can be ascertained. However, in the cases where dates can be determined, we find that by adding 2520 years to the starting date of a tribe's captivity, one comes to the date of the founding of an independent nation or kingdom.

The first Israel tribe to be conquered by the Assyrians was **Manasseh** in 745 B.C. Exactly 2520 years later, **America became a nation on July 4, 1776**. In the case of **Ephraim** we start with 721 B.C. when Samaria, the capital of the Northern Kingdom of Israel, fell to the Assyrians. Exactly 2520 years from that date, **Great Britain became a Commonwealth (Jan. 1, 1801)**. The last tribe to go into captivity was Benjamin. Remember Benjamin was "lent as a light unto Judah," so that they would be light bearers before

Judah for all times. As their captivity started later than any of the other tribes, we would expect it to end last, which proved to be the case.

The great Scottish Pyramidologist and Bible Chronologist, Dr. Adam Rutherford, F.R.G.S., told the Icelandic nation many years ago that on a certain day and certain year, they would become an independent nation. They laughed at him and said it would be impossible since they were under the control of Denmark. Exactly 2520 years from the exile of Benjamin, Iceland became an independent nation. When invited by the Icelandic Parliament to address them after their independence, Dr. Rutherford reminded them of his prediction, and many members of the Parliament acknowledged they were of Benjamin.

It is difficult to determine with certainty which Anglo-Saxon, Scandinavian, Lombard, Germanic, or Celtic nation of today is basically from which particular Israel tribe. There has been much intermingling among the tribes in their westward migrations. In God's plan of the ages, they progressively became *"many nations"* in Europe and a *"company of nations"* (the Commonwealth of Great Britain) with colonies and daughter nations. Today, certain European and Scandinavian nations appear to possess certain characteristics of the individual tribes of Israel, which may well indicate the people of those nations are predominately of that particular tribe (i.e., Denmark - Dan; Holland - Zebulun; Germany [in part] - Judah). Great Britain, although it can be identified with Ephraim, has a large infusion of Judah as well as other tribes. America, possessing the "birthright marks" of Joseph, can only be identified as modern Manasseh (the thirteenth tribe). Today the United States is comprised of *all* the thirteen tribes of Israel. This is in fulfillment of the prophecy of Jeremiah. *"In those days the house of Judah* [tribes of the Southern Kingdom] *shall walk with the house of Israel* [tribes of the Northern Kingdom], *and they shall come together out of the land of the north to the land that I have given for an inheritance* [appointed land - II Sam. 7:10] *unto your fathers."* (Jer. 3:18)

Ezekiel also prophesies the joining of Judah and Israel into one nation. *"Thus saith the Lord God; Behold, I will take the stick of Joseph, which is in the hand of Ephraim, and the tribes of Israel his fellows, and will put them with him, even with the stick of Judah, and make them one stick, and they shall be one in mine hand . . . Behold, I will take the children of Israel from among the heathen, whither they be gone, and will gather them on every side, and bring them into their own land: And I will make them one nation in the land upon the mountains of Israel; and one king* [head] *shall be king to them all; and they shall be no more two nations, neither shall they be divided into two kingdoms any more at all."* (Eze. 37:19-22)

THE BIRTH AND GROWTH OF THE "GREAT PEOPLE" OF
THE UNITED STATES OF AMERICA.

Little has been said heretofore of the portion of Israel remaining in Palestine, the "remnant" of the Southern Kingdom of Judah, after the removal of the Northern Kingdom of Israel (along with a greater part of Judah) into Assyrian captivity.

Josephus records that the portion of the nation of Judah carried into Babylonian captivity by King Nebuchadnezzar was a million and a half people. Seventy years later, when Judah was allowed to return to their homeland, although still in subjection to Persian rule, approximately forty-two thousand (Neh. 7:66) went back into Jerusalem, rebuilt the temple and set up the nation, later to be called the nation of the Jews. While in Babylon, many of the forty-two thousand intermarried with Babylonians, adopted the Babylonian financial, political and ecclesiastical systems.

Josephus further reports that many non-Israelites joined themselves to the returning Judahites. Later, Christ identified these people, also called Jews, as not of Galilee, (John 7:1-13) not of Abraham or of God, (John 8:39-47) and not His sheep. (John 10:26-30) These Jews themselves testified to not being a part of Israel by their response to Christ's words *"the truth shall make you free,"* saying they *"were never in bondage to any man."* (John 8:33) All Bible students know every tribe of Israel was in bondage in Egypt. (Deut. 5:6)

It was this mixed remnant of Judah, upon returning from the Babylon captivity in the time of Ezra and Nehemiah, that became known as the nation of the Jews; a name not applied to Judah prior to the Babylonian captivity. Included in this nation were the Edomites (known to the Greeks as Idumeans), who had occupied Jerusalem during the captivity period. King Herod the Great was an example of this, as he was of Idumean (Edomite) origin and thus not an Israelite. King Herod filled the ranks of the Sadducees with his own kind. This explains why the Sadducees did not believe in the resurrection and said there was neither angel, nor spirit. (Acts 23:8)

By the time of Christ, continued mixing with Amorites, Philistines, Canaanites, Babylonians and Hittites resulted in a racially mixed nation. From the Hittite infusion came the so-called "Jewish nose" (Hammonds World Atlas 1954 –

page 266). Modern Jewry includes a further mixing with Mongol-Turkish people (Khazar kingdom of Russia) who adopted Judaism during the 8th and 9th centuries A.D.

It is evident that among these mixed people in Israel at the time of Christ were literal descendants of Cain, for Christ said of these "Jews": *"Ye are of your father the devil [deceiver], and the lusts of your father ye will do. He was a murderer from the beginning, and abode not in the truth, because there is no truth in him. When he speaketh a lie, he speaketh of his own: for he is a liar, and the father of it. And because I tell you the truth, ye believe me not. Which of you convicteth me of sin? And if I say the truth, why do ye not believe me? He that is of God heareth God's words: ye therefore hear them not, because ye are not of God."* (John 8:44-47)

"But ye believe not, because ye are not of my sheep, as I said unto you. My sheep hear my voice, and I know them, and they follow me: And I give unto them eternal life; and they shall never perish, neither shall any man pluck them out of my hand. My Father, which gave them me, is greater than all; and no man is able to pluck them out of my Father's hand. I and my Father are one." (John 10:26-30)

John, recording God's Word in Revelation, writes, *"and I know the blasphemy of them which say they are Jews,* [of Judah] *and are not, but are the synagogue of Satan."* (Rev. 2:9) Also, *"Behold, I will make them of the synagogue of Satan, which say they are Jews,* [of Judah] *and are not, but do lie; behold, I will make them to come and worship before thy feet, and to know that I have loved thee."* (Rev. 3:9)

Christ clearly shows the separation of the people of Palestine into two classes in His answer to the question of why He spoke in parables: *"Because it is given unto you to know the mysteries of the kingdom of heaven but to them it is not given."* (Matt. 13:11)

The parable of the tares (Matt. 13:24-30) again points up two classes of people, and Christ's explanation (Matt. 13:37-43) identifies one class (the good seed) as the children of God, and the other class (the tares) as the children of the wicked one.

There are many so-called Jews today that are not descended from Abraham, but claim to be God's people "Israel," because some of them are of Judah. However, being of Judah does not necessarily mean they are still his people, for some of Judah were cut off from the promises to Israel. In Jeremiah we find God showing the prophet how He separated the bad figs (mixed seed) from the good figs of Judah who were to be Christian people. For only of them could God say, *"I will give them an heart to know me, that I am the Lord: and they shall be my people, and I will be their God: for they shall return unto me with their whole heart."* (Jer. 24:7)

Of the bad figs, God says, *"And I will deliver them to be removed into all the kingdoms of the earth for their hurt, to be a reproach and a proverb, a taunt and a curse, in all places whither I shall drive them."* (Jer. 24:9)

Keep in mind that although later historians, in writing about the people of Palestine, refer to them collectively as "Jews," there were some of all the other tribes present. They had come to help rebuild the Temple along with many Benjaminites who had been *"lent as a light unto Judah."* Christ chose all but one of His twelve disciples from the tribe of Benjamin. Thus we find the word "Jew" being applied to more than one kind of people. This has caused confusion in our understanding of the Scriptures dealing with the Jew.

To add to this confusion the translators of Scripture often mistranslated the word Jew from such words as "Ioudaios" (meaning from, or being of: as a country, Judean) and "Ioudaismos" (meaning Judaism, as accepting the Jewish faith and usages). Scripture refers to those that *"became Jews for fear of the Jews,"* (Esther 8:17) and even Paul said, *"And unto the Jews I became as a Jew, that I might gain the Jews."* (I Cor. 9:20)

As it is important to understand that in Scripture the terms "Israel," "Judah" and "Jew" are not synonymous, it is equally important to understand that the House of Israel is not synonymous with the House of Judah. The course of history is widely divergent for the peoples properly classified under each of these titles. When God speaks in prophecy to the House of Israel or the House of Judah, He does not refer to the modern "Jewish" nation of Israeli.

The prophets display meticulous care in addressing the "House of Israel" and the "House of Judah." To apply to one "House" a prophecy which refers to the other is clearly to misapply the message and confuse the issue. By failing to treat the House of Israel and the House of Judah as separate entities, the prophetic books of the Bible are set at variance with one another. Without this distinction the words of one prophet nullify the pronouncements of a fellow prophet. It makes Isaiah call into question the prophecies of Jeremiah, also causing Jeremiah to impugn the declarations of Hosea. It sets Joel against Amos, Zephaniah against Zechariah and makes Ezekiel contradict them all. Examples of such failure to make a distinction between the two Houses are found in the paraphrasing of the Living Bible which leaves the truth seeker devoid of understanding.

It is clearly shown that the House of Israel is separate from the House of Judah in the prophecy regarding the future names of each. Of the Jews (mixed Judah) it was prophesied, *"And ye shall leave* [retain] *your name* [Israel] *for a curse unto my chosen: for the Lord God shall slay thee, and call his servants by another name."* (Isaiah 65:15) This has been fulfilled. The Jews have retained the name "Israel" for *"a reproach and a proverb, a taunt and a curse,"* (Jer. 24:9) while true Israel is no

–30–

longer called by their old name. In fact, Israel is <u>blind</u> to their identity. Paul wrote, *"blindness in part is happened to Israel,"* and Isaiah wrote God's word, *"Who is blind, but my servant,"* (Isa. 42:19) and also *"thou shall be called by <u>a new name</u>, which the mouth of the Lord shall name."* (Isaiah 62:2)

God explains what that name is, *"If my people, which are called by* **MY NAME** *shall humble themselves, and pray, and seek my face, and turn from their wicked ways: then will I hear from heaven, and will forgive their sin, and will heal their land."* (II Chron. 7:14) His people are today called **Christians**; the nations of Israel are known as **Christian** nations.

There are those that claim that America is not a "Christian nation" as this would be discriminatory against other religions. However that may be, the records of the group of men that gathered in Philadelphia in 1776 – Washington, Franklin, Jefferson – show they did establish this nation under God (Christ).

> The concluding words of our National Anthem summarize the fact that the United States of America was born of a commitment to God and His principles.

Also, America has been legally declared a Christian nation many times by the Supreme Court of the United States. Foremost was the declaration February 29, 1892 in a case involving a church and certain taxes. (Holy Trinity Church vs. United States, 143 U.S. 471) The highest court in the land, after mentioning various circumstances, added the following words: *"and these and many other matters which might be noticed, add a volume of unofficial declarations to the mass of organic utterances that this is a* **CHRISTIAN NATION.**"

Let it be noted that this nation is not "anti" any religion, and it is not "hetero-religious" (many religions). It is Christian. It recognizes worship of God through Christ, the Saviour, the only Mediator between God and man. As a Christian nation, it is generous and tolerates freedom of worship. But, as a nation, it is not merely "religious," it is Christian.

It should also be noted that the framers of all the early Constitutions of the States recognized this nation as a Christian nation. This was evidenced by such points as: belief in Christ being a condition of holding public office, tax support and maintenance of public Christian schools, recognition of Sunday as the Lord's Day and recognition of Deity. This was expressed in terms such as *"Grateful to Almighty God," "So help me God"* and *"in the name of God, Amen."* Often reference was made to the God of the Old and New Testaments of the Bible.

The members of the Supreme Court of the United States take their oath of office with their hand on the Bible, the Testimony of Jesus Christ, thus recognizing His authority as being greater than theirs. Washington, when offered a crown to establish this nation as a monarchy said, *"America already has a King, God is our King."* Who was the King of Israel? God was the King of Israel, and He was the King of no other nation but Israel.

Going back to the establishment of the first colonies, we find that in 1606, King James I of England, who issued the first Charter, began with these words: *"We greatly commending, and graciously accepting of, their desires for the furtherance of so noble a work, which may be the providence of Almighty God, hereafter tend to the glory of His Divine Majesty, in propagating the Christian religion to such*

thirteen bars on our flag, and thirteen rods in our National mace.

On the reverse side of our Great Seal is shown a symbolic pyramid. Its suspended apex stone portrays the all-seeing eye of the Almighty watching over the destiny of our nation. This pyramid, identified with the Great Pyramid of Gizeh, (Isaiah 19:19-20) consists of thirteen courses of stone. Above it is written in thirteen letters, "Annuit Coeptis," (He has favored our beginnings). Altogether, there are thirteen "13"s in our heraldry.

The number thirteen was also identified with the early colonies. Massachusetts had on its emblem a pine tree with a motto above which read, *"An appeal to God,"* thirteen letters. At the base of the tree was coiled a rattlesnake beneath which was another motto, in thirteen letters, *"Don't Tread On Me."* Our first navy consisted of thirteen ships, and in many important dates in our history, both in war and peace, the number thirteen stands out preeminently.

Our flag is made up from the colors of scarlet, blue and white, the colors of Israel of old. These colors covered the table of shewbread within the Tabernacle. Red is the color of blood and signifies justice or judgment, reminding us of the shed blood of Christ for the redemption of His people Israel. White signifies purity or holiness, the color of snow. (Psalm 51:7; Isaiah 1:18) Blue, the color of the heavens, signifies love and is representative of God.

The name Manasseh means "forgetfulness" and if there has ever been a people forgetful of all their past, it is this last, this thirteenth, this Manasseh-Israel people in the United States. However, America, as prophesied of Manasseh, did become the great nation, ONE OUT OF MANY (E Pluribus Unum), and took her place in the appointed time in fulfillment of God's Covenant with Abraham.

America has yet to recognize her relationship to God, and re-institute His laws. Through the centuries Israel has usually had to be chastised into repentance. Just as God used the Assyrians to chastise Israel, He is building up the enemies of Israel-America to bring them into national repentance. Ezekiel, in chapter 38, writes of the day when the forces of Gog (antichrist) gather against Israel, saying: *"I will go up to the land of unwalled villages; I will go to them that are at rest, that dwell safely, all of them dwelling without walls, and having neither bars nor gates. To take a spoil, and to take a prey; to turn thine hand upon the desolate places that are now inhabited, and upon the people that are gathered out of the nations, which have gotten cattle and goods, that dwell in the midst of the land."* (Eze. 38:11, 12)

The people of our nation will be driven to their knees by coming events, and if they are to pray the prayer the Prophet Joel lined out for them, word for word, they must first acknowledge that they are God's servant people. Joel's instructions are: *"Let them say, Spare thy people, O Lord, and give not thine heritage to reproach, that the heathen should rule over them: wherefore should they say among the people, Where is their God"?* (Joel 2:17)

As a people, we are no more worthy than any other people. It may be, that because of our neglect of our HERITAGE, we are less worthy than any people; nevertheless, we are the descendants of Jacob-Israel, of whom God said: *"Will I be the God of all the families of Israel, and they shall be my people."* (Jer. 31:1) In spite of our unrighteousness and national rejection of God, He will not alter His word: *"Thou art my people, and they shall say, thou art my God."* (Hosea 2:23)

The day will come when America-Israel will give voice to the words spoken through the Prophet Hosea: *"Come, and let us return unto the Lord: for he hath torn, and he will heal us; he hath smitten, and he will bind us up."* (Hosea 6:1) Our God, the God of Abraham, Isaac and Jacob, will yet have the salute of our banners and the allegiance of all the people. The kingdoms of this world shall become the Kingdom of our Lord Jesus Christ, the Everlasting Father, forever and ever.

It is hoped that the truths expressed in this booklet have renewed faith in God and in the inspiration of the Bible, and have created an interest in a more complete understanding of God's dealing with the man Abraham, whose remarkable destiny the world has yet to fully consider and understand.

APPENDIX

THE MARKS OF ISRAEL

How strange it is, that with all the definite and positive assurances in the Word of God as to Israel's continuance forever as a Nation, there has never been any determined or persistent effort on the part of genuine Bible believers to find them. That they have been content to let them fade away and vanish into nothingness is surely a deep reproach on all true Christians.

There is, however, one probable explanation. It was GOD'S WILL AND PURPOSE TO HIDE THEM. While the Jews (some of whom are only a part of the House of Judah) occupied the stage, and even called themselves "Israel," God could work unhindered with and in "Lost Israel," till he had finished his predetermined work, and without them knowing they were THE PEOPLE of the Book. Only as Israel's time of punishment had run out, with the whole of God's purposes at the point of complete fulfillment, was the identity of Israel to become known.

However, it is a matter of inspired record that God placed "marks" on His people Israel. During the Christian dispensation, Lost Israel was to possess these marks of identification. So then, if we can discover the nations and people with Israel's marks, we have found the people whom God chose to serve Him to be a channel of blessing to all mankind. The God-given marks are very many, and while the following list is not exhaustive, they constitute a chain of evidence utterly impossible to ignore.

One race, and one race alone, has all these marks. Nations within this race may have only a portion of them, but the race as a whole has them all. With a few exceptions, Joseph (the birthright nation) was the recipient of them all. By inheritance, his two sons, Ephraim (Great Britain) and Manasseh (U.S.A.) will be found possessing them all.

While Israelites remain in other countries, America is the home of millions of all the thirteen tribes (one out of many), and thus is representative of the whole House of Jacob. We are bound by Israel's responsibilities; fulfilling Israel's destiny. The MARKS are on us everywhere: in our NAME; in our SABBATH; in our INSTITUTIONS; in our PHILANTHROPY; in our COMMERCE; in our WEALTH; in our MINES; in our AGRICULTURE; in our CHURCHES; in our MISSIONARY ENTERPRISES; in our ARMED FORCES; in our POSSESSION OF THE BIBLE. All are BIRTHMARKS, which neither time, nor the ages, nor even our sin can wipe out.

1. **Israel to be a great and mighty nation.**
   Gen. 12:2; 18:18; Deut. 4:7,8.

2. **Israel to have multitudinous seed.**
   Gen. 13:16; 15:5; 22:17; 24:60; 26:4,24; 28:3,14; 32:12; 49:22; Isa. 10:22; Hos. 1:10; Zech. 10:7,8.

3. **Israel to spread abroad to the West, East, North, and South.**
   Gen. 28:14; Isa. 42:5,6.

4. **Israel to have a new home.**
   II Sam. 7:10; I Chron. 17:9.

5. **Israel's home to be northwest of Palestine.**
   Isa. 49:12; Jer. 3:18.

6. **Israel to live in islands and coasts of the earth.**
   Isa. 41:1; 49:1-3; 51:5; Jer. 31:7-10.

7. **Israel to become a company of nations.**
   Gen. 17:4-6,15,16; 35:11; 48:19; Eph. 2:12.

8. **Israel to have a Davidic King (a perpetual monarchy within Israel).**
   II Sam. 7:13,19; I Chron. 22:10; II Chron. 13:5; Psa. 89:20,37; Eze. 37:24; Jer. 33:17,21,26.

9. **Israel to colonize and spread abroad.**
Gen. 28:14; 49:22; Deut. 32:8; 33:17; Psa. 2:8; Isa. 26:15; 27:6; 54:2; Zech. 10:8,9.

10. **Israel to colonize the desolate place of the earth.**
Isa. 35:1; 43:19,20; 49:8; 54:3; 58:11,12.

11. **Israel to lose a colony, then expand, demanding more room.**
Isa. 49:19, 20.

12. **Israel to have all the land needed.**
Deut. 32:8.

13. **Israel to be the first among the nations.**
Gen. 27:29; 28:13; Jer. 31:7.

14. **Israel to continue as a nation forever.**
II Sam. 7:16,24,29; I Chron. 17:22-27; Jer. 31:35-37.

15. **Israel's home to be invincible by outside forces.**
II Sam. 7:10; Isa. 41:11-14.

16. **Israel to be undefeatable – defended by God.**
Num. 24:8,9; Isa. 15-17; Micah 5:8,9.

17. **Israel to be God's instruments in destroying evil.**
Jer. 51:20; 51:19-24; Dan. 2:34,35.

18. **Israel to have a land of great mineral wealth.**
Gen. 49:25,26; Deut. 8:9; 33:15-19.

19. **Israel to have a land of great agricultural wealth.**
Gen. 27:28; Deut. 8:7,9; 28:11; 33:13,14,28.

20. **Israel to be rich by trading.**
Isa. 60:5-11; 61:6.

21. **Israel to be envied and feared by all nations.**
Deut. 2:25; 4:8; 28:10; Isa. 43:4; 60:10,12; Micah 7:16,17; Jer. 33:9.

22. **Israel to lend to other nations, borrowing of none.**
Deut. 15:6; 28:12.

23. **Israel to have a new name.**
Isa. 62:2; 65:15; Hos. 2:17.

24. **Israel to have a new language.**
Isa. 28:11 (The Bible, by means of which God speaks now to Israel, is English not Hebrew.)

25. **Israel to possess the gates of her enemies.**
Gen. 22:17.

26. **Israel to find the aborigines diminishing before them.**
Deut. 33:17; Isa. 60:12; Jer. 31:7-10.

27. **Israel to have control of the seas.**
Deut. 33:19; Num. 24:7; Psa. 89:25; Isa. 60:5
(F. Fenton translates this last, "when rolls up to you all the wealth of the sea." That could not be unless Israel controlled it.)

28. **Israel to have a new religion (New Covenant).**
Heb. 8:10-13; 9:17; Matt. 10:5-7; Luke 1:77; 2:32; 22:20; John 11:49-52; Gal. 3:13.

29. **Israel to lose all trace of her lineage.**
Isa. 42:16-19; Hos. 1:9,10; 2:6; Rom. 11:25.

30. **Israel to keep the Sabbath forever (one day in seven set aside).**
Ex. 31:13,16,17; Isa. 58:13,14.

31. **Israel to be called the sons of God (i.e., accept Christianity).**
Hos. 1:10-11.

32. **Israel to be a people saved by the Lord.**
Deut. 33:27-29; Isa. 41:8-14; 43:1-8; 44:1-3; 49:25,26;
52:1-12; 55:3-10,13; Jer. 46:27,28; Eze. 34:10-16;
Hos. 2:23; 13:9-14; 14:4,6.

33. **Israel to be custodians of the Oracles (Scriptures) of God.**
Psa. 147:19,21; Isa. 59:21.

34. **Israel to carry the Gospel to all the world.**
Gen. 28:14; Isa. 43:10-12 (witnesses), 21; Micah 5:7.

35. **Israel to be kind to the poor and set slaves free.**
Deut. 15:7,11; Psa. 72:4; Isa. 42:7; 49:9; 58:6.

36. **Israel to be the heir of the world.**
Rom. 4:13.

37. **Israel to be God's Glory.**
Isa. 46:13; 49:3; 60:1,2.

38. **Israel to possess God's Holy Spirit as well as His Word.**
Isa. 44:3; 59:21; Hag. 2:5.

39. **Israel to be God's Heritage, formed by God forever.**
Deut. 4:20; 7:6; 14:2; II Sam. 7:23; I Kings 8:51,53;
Isa. 43:21; 54:5-10; Hos. 2:19,23; Joel 2:27;
Micah 7:14-18.

40. **Israel is the nation appointed to bring glory to God.**
Isa. 41:8-16; 43:10,21; 44:23; 49:3.

"YE SEED OF ISRAEL'S CHOSEN RACE,
YE RANSOMED FROM THE FALL,
HAIL HIM WHO SAVES YOU BY HIS GRACE,
AND CROWN HIM LORD OF ALL."

NAMES GOD GAVE TO ISRAEL

ANCIENTS (Isa. 3:14; 24:23; Jer. 19:1; Ezek. 7:26; 8:2).

ANOINTED (I Chr. 16:22; Ps. 2:2; 105:15; Hab. 3:13; Zech. 4:14).

BATTLE-AXE (Jer. 51:20).

BELOVED (Ps. 60:5; Isa. 5:1; Rom. 11:28).

DEARLY BELOVED (Jer. 31:20).

BETROTHED (Hos. 2:19).

BLESSED (Gen. 12:2; 14:19; 18:18; Deut. 7:14; Ps. 33:12; Isa. 51:2; 61:9; 65:23).

BLESSING (Gen. 12:2,3; 28:4; Deut. 33:1,16; Ps. 3:8; Isa. 19:24; 65:8; Zech. 8:13; Gal. 3:14; Heb. 6:14).

BRANCH (Ps. 80:15; Isa. 6:2; 60:21).

BRIDE (Isa. 62:5; Jer. 33:2; Joel 2:16).

CHIEF OF NATIONS (Jer. 31:7).

CHILDREN (Deut. 14:1; I Chr. 16:13; 82:6; Isa. 49:23; Joel 2:23).

CHILDREN OF ZION (Ps. 149:2).

LOVED CHILD (Hos. 11:1).

PLEASANT CHILD (Jer. 31:20).

CHOSEN (Deut. 7:6; 14:2; Ps. 105:6; 135:4; Isa. 41:9; 43:10; 47:10).

CHOSEN GENERATION (I Pet. 2:9).

CONGREGATION (Num. 16:3; Ps. 68:10; 74:2; Joel 2:16).

CONSECRATED (Ex. 32:29; I Chr. 29:5; II Chr. 29:5; II Chr. 29:31; Eze. 43:26; Micah 4:13).

DELIGHT (Deut. 10:15).

DEW FROM THE LORD (Micah 5:7).

ROYAL DIADEM (Isa. 62:3).

DOMINION (Ps. 117:4; 68:34).

ETERNAL EXCELLENCY (Isa. 60:15).

SWORD OF EXCELLENCY (Deut. 33:29).

FIRSTBORN (Ex. 4:22; Jer. 31:9).

FIRSTFRUITS OF INCREASE (Jer. 2:3).

FLOCK (Isa. 40:2; Jer. 13:17,20; 23:2; 31:10; Eze. 36:38; Micah 7:14; Zech. 9:16; I Pet. 5:2).

FOUNTAIN (Deut. 33:28; Ps. 68:26).

FRUIT (Isa. 27:6; Eze. 17:8; Hos. 14:8; Matt. 21:43).

WATERED GARDEN (Isa. 58:2; Jer. 31:12).

GLORIFIED (Isa. 26:15; 44:23; 40:55; 60:9).

GLORY (Isa. 43:7; 46:13; 60:7; Luke 2:32).

CROWN OF GLORY (Isa. 62:3; Zec. 9:16).

HEIRS OF THE PROMISE (Heb. 6:17).

HEIRS OF SALVATION (Heb. 1:14).

HEIRS OF THE WORLD (Rom. 4:13).

HERITAGE (Isa. 54:17; Joel 2:17; 3:2; Micah 7:14,18; I Pet. 5:3).

SPIRITUAL HOUSE (Eph. 2:21,22; I Pet. 2:5).

INHERITANCE (Deut. 9:26,29; I Kings 8:51; Ps. 33:12; 68:9; 106:5; Isa. 19:25; 68:17).

PEOPLE OF INHERITANCE (Deut. 4:20).

ROD OF INHERITANCE (Ps. 74:2; Jer. 11:16; 51:19).

JEWELS (Isa. 62:3; Mal. 3:17).

JOY OF MANY NATIONS (Isa. 60:15).

KINGS (Isa. 49:7,23).

KINGDOM OF GOD (Matt. 21:43).

KINGDOM (Ex. 19:6; Num. 24:7; Deut. 17:20).

LAW GIVERS (Ps. 78:5; 147:19; Isa. 42:4; 51:7).

LIGHT (Isa. 51:4; 60:3; Luke 2:32).

GREAT LION (Num. 23:24; Micah 5:8).

YOUNG LIONS (Isa. 5:29; Eze. 19: 2; 38:13).

LOT (Deut. 32:9).

EVERLASTING LOVE (Deut. 7:8; Jer. 31:3; Hos. 11:1).

MIGHTY MEN (Joel 3:9; Nah. 2:3; Zech. 10:5).

VALIANT MEN (Nah. 2:3).

MERCHANTS OF TARSHISH (Eze. 38:13).

MESSENGERS (Isa. 14:32; 42:19; 44:26).

MESSENGERS OF THE COVENANT (Mal. 3:1).

MINISTERS (Isa. 61:6).

BLESSED NATION (Ps. 33:12).

EVERLASTING NATION (Gen. 17:5,6; I Chr. 17:21,22; II Sam. 7:23,24; Eze. 37:12-28; Luke 1:33,55).

GREAT NATION (Gen. 12:2; Deut. 4:6,8).

GREAT AND MIGHTY NATION (Gen. 18:18).

HOLY NATION (Ex. 19:6; I Pet. 2:9).

ISLAND NATION (Isa. 24:14; 41:1; 43:4,5,10; 49:1,19; Jer. 33:8; 31:10).

MIGHTY NATION (Isa. 26:2).

NATION WHOSE GOD IS THE LORD (Ps. 33:12; 144:15).

NATION & COMPANY OF NATIONS (Gen. 35:11).

RIGHTEOUS NATION (Ps. 118:19,20; Isa. 26:2; Hos. 2:19).

STRONG NATION (Isa. 60:22; Micah 4:7).

WEALTHY NATION (Jer. 49:31).

ACCEPTED ONES (Isa. 56:7; Eze. 20:41; I Pet. 2:5).

GATHERED ONES (Isa. 27:12; 54:7; 56:8; Jer. 29:14; 31:10; Eze. 28:25).

LOVED ONES (Deut. 4:27).

MARRIED ONES (Jer. 3:14; Hos. 2:19).

REVIVED ONES (Ps. 85:6; Hos. 6:2).

SANCTIFIED ONES (Isa. 13:3; Eze. 20:41; 39:27).

SAVED ONES (Deut. 33:29; Ps. 44:7; Isa. 45:22; Luke 1:71).

OUTCASTS (Ps. 147:2; Isa. 11:13).

PASTURE (Ps. 95:2).

PEOPLE OF THE GOD OF ABRAHAM (Ps. 47:9).

HIS PEOPLE (Ex. 6:7; Deut. 32:9; II Chr. 2:2; Ps. 78:71; Luke 7:16).

PEOPLE CHOSEN FOR HIS OWN INHERITANCE (Ps. 33:12).

COLONIZING PEOPLE (Isa. 35:1; 49:8).

COVENANT PEOPLE (Gen. 17:7; 22:16; 105:8,9,10; Eze. 37:26; Luke 1:73; Heb. 6:13).

HOLY PEOPLE (Deut. 14:2; 26:18; I Pet. 2:9).

PUSHING PEOPLE (Num. 23:22; Deut. 33:17; Isa. 34:7).

PURCHASED PEOPLE (Ex. 15:6; Ps. 74:2).

RIGHTEOUS PEOPLE (Isa. 60:21).

SEPARATE PEOPLE (Num. 23:9; Deut. 33:28).

SPECIAL PEOPLE (Deut. 7:6).

PLEASANT PLANT (Isa. 5:7).

PLANTING (Isa. 61:3).

PORTION (Deut. 32:9).

PURCHASED POSSESSION (Eph. 1:14).

PRAISE (Deut. 26:19; Isa. 43:21).

KINGDOM OF PRIESTS (Ex. 19:6).

HOLY PRIESTHOOD (I Pet. 2:5,9).

ROYAL PRIESTHOOD (I Pet. 2:9).

PRIEST OF THE LORD (Isa. 61:6).

RANSOMED (Isa. 35:10; Jer. 31:2; Hos. 13:14).

REDEEMED (Isa. 44:23; 48:20; 62:12; Jer. 31:2).

REJOICING (Isa. 62:5; 65:13,19; 66:10,14; Jer. 32:42).

REMNANT (Isa. 46:3; Jer. 23:3).

RESIDUE (Isa. 28:5; Zech. 8:2).

TREES OF RIGHTEOUSNESS (Isa. 61:3).

SAINTS (Deut. 33:3; Ps. 50:5; 85:8; 97:10; 147:14; Dan. 7:27).

SANCTIFIED (Lev. 21:23; Isa. 13:3; Eze. 20:41; 39:27; Heb. 10:14.

SANCTUARY (Ex. 15:17; 25:8; Ps. 114:2; Isa. 43:28; Eze. 37:28).

SEED THE LORD HATH BLESSED (Isa. 61:9).

SERVANTS (Ps. 69:36; Isa. 41:8,9; 43:21; 65:9,13,15).

SHEEP (Ps. 74:1; 95:7; 100:3; Jer. 31:10; Eze. 34:11,12).

LOST SHEEP (Jer. 50:6; Matt. 10:6; 15:24).

SHIELDS OF THE EARTH (Ps. 47:9).

SHIELD OF HELP (Deut. 33:29; Ps. 115:9,10,11).

SHIELD OF MIGHT MEN (Nah. 2:3).

SHIPS OF TARSHISH (Isa. 60:9).

SON (Ex. 4:22; Isa. 42:6; 45:2; Hos. 1:10; 11:1; John 1:12; II Cor. 6:18).

DEAR SON (Jer. 31:20).

LIVELY STONES (Eph. 2:21,22; I Pet. 2:5).

STRENGTH (Ps. 60:7; 68:35; Deut. 33:17).

TABERNACLE (Lev. 26:11,12; Eze. 37:27; Amos 9:11; Acts 7:44,46; 15:10).

TEMPLE (I Cor. 3:16,17; II Cor. 6:16; Eph. 2:21,22).

TESTIMONY (Ps. 78:5; 132:12; 147:19).

PECULIAR TREASURE (Ex. 18:5; Ps. 135:4).

GREEN OLIVE TREE (Jer. 11:16; Rom. 11:17).

TRIBES (Ps. 122:4; Isa. 49:6; 68:17).
THRONE (Deut.17:18; II Sam. 7:13; I Chr. 22:10; Ps. 89:4;
    Jer. 14:21; Eze. 43:7).
VINE (Ps. 80:8; Jer. 6:9; Eze. 17:6; Hos. 14:7).
NOBLE VINE (Jer. 2:21).
GOODLY VINE (Eze. 17:8).
VINEYARD (Ps. 80:15; Isa. 5; Jer. 12:10).
VIRGIN (Jer. 31:4,21; Amos 5:2).
WANDERERS (Hos. 9:17).
WEAPONS OF WAR (Jer. 51:20).
WITNESSES (Isa. 43:10,12; 44:8).

"Hearken to me, ye that follow after righteousness, ye that seek the Lord: Look unto the rock whence ye are hewn, and to the hole of the pit whence ye are digged. Look unto Abraham your father, and unto Sarah that bare you: for I called him alone, and blessed him, and increased him . . . . Hearken unto me, my people; and give ear unto me, O my nation."

Isaiah 51:1-2,4

This "Outline" of the Identity of God's people as revealed by the study of God's Covenant with Abraham was compiled as a guide-line for study. No infallibility is claimed for the opinions expressed herein. Much research and study is still necessary before every facet of this wonderful truth is known in all its perfection. This remains to be done by honest and sincere searchers for truth, who may not only correct errors but add to our understanding of God's truth. To gain this knowledge – *Search the Scriptures*.

E. Raymond Capt

> "Our eyes are holden that we cannot see things that stare us in the face until the hour arrives when the mind is ripened. Then we behold them, and the time when we saw them not is like a dream."
>
> (R. W. Emerson)